TOTAL
FOOTBALL

BY BARRY WILNER

SportsZone

An Imprint of Abdo Publishing
www.abdopublishing.com

abdopublishing.com

Published by Abdo Publishing, a division of ABDO, PO Box 398166, Minneapolis, Minnesota 55439. Copyright © 2017 by Abdo Consulting Group, Inc. International copyrights reserved in all countries. No part of this book may be reproduced in any form without written permission from the publisher. SportsZone™ is a trademark and logo of Abdo Publishing.

Printed in the United States of America, North Mankato, Minnesota
092016
012017

THIS BOOK CONTAINS RECYCLED MATERIALS

Cover Photos: Kathy Willens/AP Images, foreground; Shutterstock Images, background
Interior Photos: Shutterstock Images, 1; Eric Gay/AP Images, 4–5; Tony Tomsic/AP Images, 6, 8, 32; Kevin Dietsch/UPI/Newscom, 10–11; Damian Dovarganes/AP Images, 12; AP Images, 14–15, 17, 18, 28–29, 30; NFL Photos/AP Images, 20–21, 27; Elaine Thompson/AP Images, 22; San Francisco Examiner/AP Images, 24–25; Greg Trott/AP Images, 35; Mitchell Reibel/AI Wire Photo Service/Newscom, 36–37; SportsChrome/Newscom, 38; Tom DiPace/AP Images, 40; Vernon Biever/NFL Photos/AP Images, 42–43; Atkins/AP Images, 45; Rusty Kennedy/AP Images, 46–47; Andy Blenkush/Cal Sport Media/AP Images, 48; HH/AP Images, 50–51; Perry Knotts/AP Images, 53; David Goldman/AP Images, 54–55; Debby Wong/Shutterstock Images, 56; Andrew Rich/iStockphoto, 58–59; Paul Jasienski/AP Images, 61

Editor: Patrick Donnelly
Series Designer: Jake Nordby

Publisher's Cataloging-in-Publication Data

Names: Wilner, Barry, author.
Title: Total football / by Barry Wilner.
Description: Minneapolis, MN : Abdo Publishing, 2017. | Series: Total sports |
    Includes bibliographical references and index.
Identifiers: LCCN 2016945393 | ISBN 9781680785036 (lib. bdg.) | ISBN
    9781680798319 (ebook)
Subjects: LCSH: Football--Juvenile literature.
Classification: DDC 796.332--dc23
LC record available at http://lccn.loc.gov/2016945393

CONTENTS

SUPER BOWL SUPERSTARS

The Super Bowl is America's party. It's practically a national holiday.

The championship game of the National Football League (NFL) is a big deal. Millions of people even watch the halftime show and the TV commercials. The cheapest game tickets cost approximately $850 in 2016.

But it wasn't always that way. In 1966 the NFL decided to join with the rival American Football League (AFL). The winners of each league would play in the AFL-NFL World Championship Game.

Drew Brees holds the Lombardi Trophy after the New Orleans Saints won the Super Bowl in February 2010.

It's the game we now call the Super Bowl. The first one was played in the Los Angeles Memorial Coliseum.

The NFL champions, the Green Bay Packers, were a great team. They trounced the AFL's Kansas City Chiefs 35–10. But the sports world didn't pay much attention. Only two-thirds of the available tickets were sold. Other sports championships were more popular, especially baseball's World Series.

The first Super Bowl was televised by both CBS and NBC.

The Packers returned the next year and again throttled the AFL champion. They routed the Oakland Raiders 33–14 in Miami. This time the stadium was filled. But after those two Packers wins, people began wondering if an AFL team could

Joe Namath and the New York Jets pulled off the first Super Bowl upset.

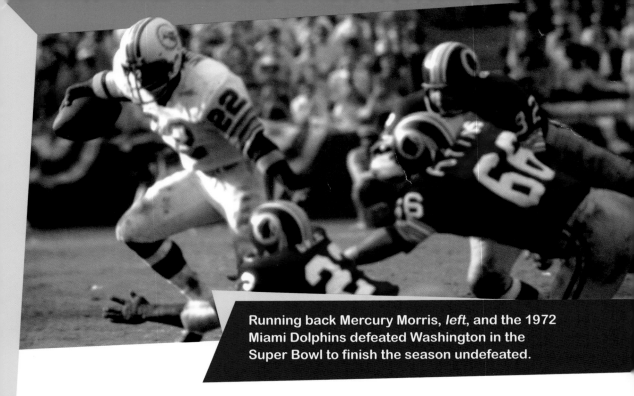

Running back Mercury Morris, *left*, and the 1972 Miami Dolphins defeated Washington in the Super Bowl to finish the season undefeated.

ever beat an NFL club. That changed in shocking fashion in 1969.

The NFL champion Baltimore Colts were expected to thrash the AFL's New York Jets. The Colts were favored by three touchdowns. New York's brash young quarterback, "Broadway" Joe Namath, guaranteed a Jets win a few days before the game. That brought added attention to the game. Then Namath led the Jets to the biggest upset in pro football history. They beat the mighty Colts 16–7.

The Super Bowl had finally become super.

The popularity of the NFL's biggest game took off from there. Great teams won it. The 1972 Miami Dolphins went 17–0. They remain the only undefeated Super Bowl champs. Great teams also lost it. In 2007 the New England Patriots won their first 18 games. But they lost to the New York Giants in the Super Bowl.

Some teams became dynasties. In the 1970s the Pittsburgh Steelers won four Super Bowls in six years. The San Francisco 49ers won four championships in the 1980s. The Dallas Cowboys won three titles in four years in the 1990s. New England did the same in the 2000s.

DIG IN!

Chowing down at parties has become a big part of the Super Bowl tradition. Americans eat more food on Super Bowl Sunday than on any other day of the year besides Thanksgiving. Fans eat approximately 100 million pounds of avocado (used in guacamole) and more than 1 billion chicken wings that day.

And one team, the Buffalo Bills, went to four straight Super Bowls from 1991–94. But they lost them all.

2

GOING
BOWLING

On January 12, 2015, Ohio State won the first College Football Playoff.

For years the top level of college football used polls to determine its champion. Sports writers voted in the Associated Press poll. Coaches voted in the United Press International (and later, *USA Today*) poll. Sometimes the writers and coaches didn't agree. Two teams had to share the title. Finally, a plan came along that allowed the teams to decide it on the field.

Ohio State's Ezekiel Elliott, *15*, and Corey Smith celebrate during the first College Football Playoff National Championship.

Parade floats and marching bands are part of the many traditions that bring visitors to Pasadena, California, every New Year's Day.

The voting system was a strange way to name a champion. But it was done that way for an important reason. College football wanted to protect the tradition of its bowl games.

Those bowl games began with the Rose Bowl. It's still known as "The Granddaddy of Them All." It was first played in 1902 in Pasadena, California. The president of the Tournament of Roses parade wanted to make the game an annual event. At first it didn't work. Michigan beat Stanford 49–0, and the game was discontinued for 13 years.

College football drew more interest over time. The Rose Bowl was held again in 1916. It has been played every year since.

Soon other cities began to realize how many fans traveled to Pasadena to support their teams. They wanted a similar draw to boost their economies. So other bowl games were born.

First came the Festival of Palms Bowl in Miami in 1933. It soon got a new name: the Orange Bowl. The Sugar Bowl followed in New Orleans in 1935. Then the Sun Bowl in El Paso, Texas, in 1936 and the Cotton Bowl in Dallas in 1937. Bowl games have been a favorite tradition of college football fans ever since.

WHAT'S IN A NAME?

Everyone knows what a rose is. Cotton and sugar are familiar products, too. But some bowl games have had much wilder names. Try the Poulan Weed-Eater Independence Bowl. Or the Astro Bluebonnet Bowl. Or the Beef O'Brady's Bowl. There even once was a Boardwalk Bowl. It was played indoors in Atlantic City, New Jersey.

3

THE EARLY DAYS

College students from Rutgers and Princeton played the first game in 1869. Rutgers won 6–4. The Rutgers student newspaper called the event "foot-ball." Approximately 100 people watched.

But it didn't look much like the football that's played today. Each touchdown was worth one point. There were 25 players on each side. The field was 120 yards by 75 yards. The goal posts were 24 feet apart. And the ball was round and made of rubber. It could only be kicked, batted with the hands, or headed like a soccer ball.

Yale takes on Carlisle at New York's Polo Grounds in 1907 in a game that looks far different from modern football.

Rules began to change over the years. So did the ball. It became more of an oval shape. Leather became the most common material used to make it. And with leather came stitching, or laces, making it easier to throw.

But the games became very rough. In the early 1900s lots of players were getting hurt. Some were even killed during games. President Teddy Roosevelt was a football fan. He wanted the game to survive. But he knew it had to change. Roosevelt met with coaches and officials from some of the most powerful colleges. He urged them to make football safer.

The coaches helped push through rule changes. Perhaps the most important change was making the forward pass legal. That helped spread out the players on the field. They also

Alabama (2011–12) was the first team to win undisputed back-to-back national titles since Nebraska (1994–95).

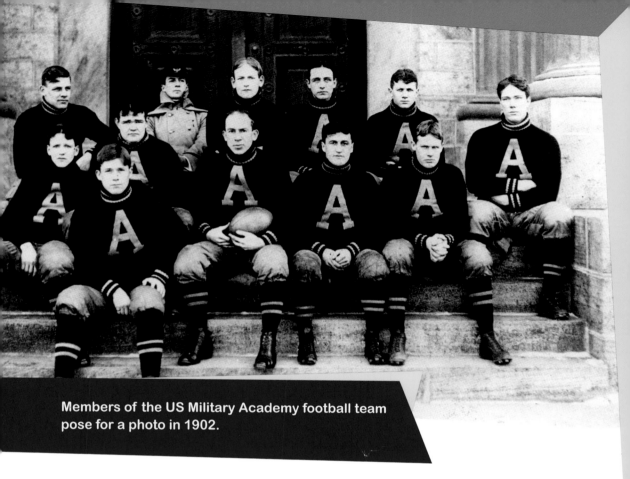

Members of the US Military Academy football team pose for a photo in 1902.

established penalties to stop dangerous plays. Those changes worked. Soon more schools were playing football, and the sport looked more like what it is today.

Some of the greatest teams through the first 50 years of college football were in the East. Army and Navy were dominant. Fordham and Rutgers popularized the game in the New York/New Jersey region. Harvard, Princeton, and Yale were national powers from the Ivy League.

The center of power began moving west. Soon Michigan, Minnesota, and Ohio State were strong. Notre Dame and Nebraska were other Midwestern powerhouses.

In the South, Alabama, Auburn, Georgia Tech, and Tennessee developed tough programs. Texas, Oklahoma, and Arkansas emerged in the Southwest. Southern California, Washington, and Stanford were strong on the Pacific coast.

Pro football became more popular as college players moved into the NFL. In the 1950s and 60s, the Chicago Bears, Green Bay Packers, and New York Giants were among the most famous and popular teams. Before long, football became America's No. 1 sport.

AIR ATTACK

Not many teams used the forward pass in football's early days. That changed in 1913 when Notre Dame played Army. Notre Dame quarterback Gus Dorais passed to receiver Knute Rockne time after time. Army had no idea how to stop it, and Notre Dame won 35–13. Passing was here to stay.

Knute Rockne, *left*, was a legendary player and coach at Notre Dame.

4

GREAT PLAYS

Some of football's greatest plays won playoff games or even championships. Some even have fun nicknames.

For example, "The Immaculate Reception" gave the Pittsburgh Steelers a shocking upset in 1972. The Steelers trailed the Oakland Raiders 7–6 in the final seconds of their American Football Conference (AFC) playoff game. On fourth down, quarterback Terry Bradshaw heaved the ball downfield to teammate Frenchy Fuqua. Raiders safety Jack Tatum blasted Fuqua as the ball arrived near midfield.

Franco Harris outruns the Oakland Raiders defense to score an unlikely touchdown on the play known as "The Immaculate Reception."

Giants wide receiver David Tyree, *left*, pins the ball to his helmet as Patriots safety Rodney Harrison tries to break up the pass.

Trailing the play, Pittsburgh's Franco Harris scooped up the ball before it hit the ground. He sprinted down the sideline for a 60-yard touchdown to win the game.

The Tennessee Titans also came up with an amazing play to win a playoff game after the 1999 season. The Buffalo Bills took a 16–15 lead on a field goal with 16 seconds left in the game. Tennessee's Lorenzo Neal fielded Buffalo's kickoff. He pitched the ball to teammate Frank Wycheck at the Titans 25-yard line. Wycheck turned to the left sideline. Then he threw the ball across the field to Kevin Dyson.

Dyson caught it and sped 75 yards to the end zone. The Bills argued that Wycheck's throw across the field was a forward pass, which would be illegal. But replays showed Wycheck's pass was a lateral. The touchdown gave Tennessee a 22–16 win on a play known as "The Music City Miracle."

The New York Giants used "The Helmet Catch" to shock the New England Patriots in the Super Bowl after the 2007 season. New England led late in the game. New York quarterback Eli Manning lofted a desperation pass downfield. Receiver David Tyree leapt high to make the catch. Tyree pinned the ball against his helmet with his right hand as he fell. A few plays later, the Giants scored a touchdown to win the game.

THE CATCH

The San Francisco 49ers reached their first Super Bowl on "The Catch." The 49ers trailed the Dallas Cowboys late in the 1981 National Football Conference (NFC) championship game. Quarterback Joe Montana scrambled to his right. He flung the ball toward the back of the end zone. Wide receiver Dwight Clark leapt as high as he could. He came down with the ball for the game-winning touchdown.

5 STRANGE PLAYS

Sometimes things don't go as planned on the football field. Roy Riegels, Jim Marshall, and Garo Yepremian know all about that.

Georgia Tech faced California in the 1929 Rose Bowl. Riegels, California's star linebacker, scooped up a fumble and began running toward the goal line. He didn't realize that he was running the wrong way. Teammates yelled at him to stop. One of them finally caught him at California's 1-yard line.

Georgia Tech scored a safety on the next play. Tech went on to win the game 8–7. And for the

Vikings defensive end Jim Marshall runs the wrong way with a fumble in a 1964 game in San Francisco.

rest of his life, a great football player was called "Wrong-Way" Riegels because of one play.

A similar play happened in the NFL. Marshall was a starting defensive end for the Minnesota Vikings for 19 seasons. But he made headlines for running 60 yards the wrong way with a fumble against San Francisco in 1964. Unlike Riegels, Marshall outran his teammates. When he crossed the goal line, the 49ers were awarded a safety. Marshall said he didn't realize what he had done until a 49ers player thanked him in the end zone.

Yepremian was the kicker on the undefeated Dolphins of 1972. In the Super Bowl, Miami led Washington 14–0 early in the fourth quarter. Yepremian lined up to boot a field goal. But the kick

WHAT'S A SAFETY?

A safety is a scoring play that earns two points for the defense. It can happen when a player gets tackled in his own end zone with the ball. If a fumble or blocked punt goes out of bounds in the end zone, that's also a safety. The defensive team gets two points for a safety. Plus the other team also has to kick the ball to them.

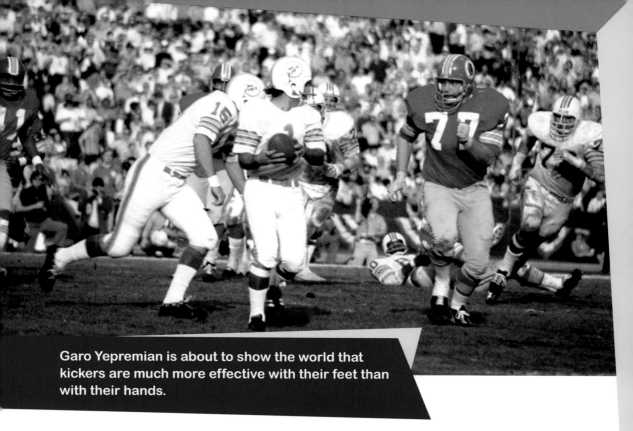

Garo Yepremian is about to show the world that kickers are much more effective with their feet than with their hands.

was blocked. The ball bounced back to Yepremian. He picked it up and tried to pass.

But Yepremian made his living with his leg, not his arm. The ball slipped through his hands and popped straight up into the air. Washington's Mike Bass caught it and ran 49 yards for a touchdown.

Miami held on to win 14–7. But Yepremian's miscue would become one of football's most famous bloopers.

6 OFFENSIVE STARS

For many football fans, offense is the name of the game. They love seeing points put up on the scoreboard. And they cheer loudly for the players who score them.

Football was a run-first game in the early days. Its biggest stars were mostly running backs. One of the most famous was Red Grange. He was known as "The Galloping Ghost." Grange was a three-time All-American at the University of Illinois. He attracted big crowds wherever he played.

Red Grange was one of the game's earliest stars at both the college and pro levels.

His popularity carried over to the NFL. Grange signed with the Chicago Bears the day after his final college game. He tore through defenses and filled the stadiums. Fans nearly broke down the fences trying to get into one game in New York to see him play. Grange was the NFL's first true superstar. He made the Hall of Fame on both the college and pro levels.

Through 2016 Jan Stenerud was the only kicker in the Pro Football Hall of Fame.

Other big-play runners made names for themselves in college football, too. Bronko Nagurski (Minnesota), Tom Harmon (Michigan), and Nile Kinnick (Iowa) were stars in the 1920s and 30s. In the 1940s, Doc Blanchard and Glenn Davis (Army), Doak Walker (Southern Methodist), and Charley Trippi (Georgia) were big stars. Howard "Hopalong" Cassidy (Ohio State), Paul Hornung

Paul Hornung of Notre Dame was one of football's golden boys in the 1950s.

Jim Brown breaks a tackle against the Eagles in a 1965 game.

(Notre Dame), and Billy Cannon (Louisiana State) were campus heroes in the 1950s.

The best might have been Jim Brown. He starred at Syracuse University. He joined the Cleveland Browns in 1957. Brown played nine years in Cleveland. He led the NFL in rushing eight times.

Brown was the NFL's career rushing leader when he retired in 1965. He yielded that title to Walter Payton of the Chicago Bears in 1984. Longtime Dallas Cowboy Emmitt Smith passed Payton in 2002. Smith will be hard to beat. He left the game with 18,355 career rushing yards. Only Payton and Barry Sanders have come within 4,000 yards of that mark.

As the passing game gained prominence in the NFL, so did the fame of star quarterbacks. Sid Luckman became one of the league's first great passers with the Bears in the 1940s. Washington's Sammy Baugh was a brilliant passer. He also punted and played defense. Otto Graham led the Browns to the playoffs in all of his 10 seasons. John Unitas was an icon with the Baltimore Colts.

HEISMAN HEROES

The Heisman Trophy has been given to the top college football player every season since 1935. Michigan's Charles Woodson in 1997 became the only primarily defensive player to win it. The trophy is named after John Heisman. He was a legendary coach at Pennsylvania University. Heisman was the first coach to have his quarterback yell "Hike!" to signal the start of a play.

In the 1960s Bart Starr won five NFL titles, including the first two Super Bowls, with the Packers. Terry Bradshaw won four Super Bowls with the Steelers in the 1970s. Joe Montana won four titles with the 49ers in the 1980s. Tom Brady won his fourth Super Bowl with the Patriots after the 2014 season.

Chuck Bednarik played center and middle linebacker for the Philadelphia Eagles from 1949 to 1962.

Many experts call Jerry Rice the greatest wide receiver of all time. He was teammate Joe Montana's favorite target. Rice caught 1,549 passes for nearly 22,895 yards. And he scored 197 touchdowns in the NFL. No player has come close to breaking any of those records.

Other great receivers thrived as the NFL became more pass-oriented. Lance Alworth of the San Diego Chargers was a star in the pass-happy AFL. The duo of Lynn Swann

Joe Montana, *left*, and Jerry Rice were a potent combination for the San Francisco 49ers in the 1980s.

and John Stallworth teamed with Bradshaw on all four of the Steelers' Super Bowl teams. Randy Moss and Cris Carter put up some huge numbers for the Vikings in the late 1990s. And no tight end caught more passes in his career than Tony Gonzalez. Gonzalez made 1,325 receptions in 12 years with the Chiefs and five years with the Falcons. He is second only to Rice on the career list.

7 DEFENSIVE STUDS

For all the great players who threw, caught, and ran with the ball, there have been stars who tried to stop them. Many were colorful characters as well as intimidating defenders. Deacon Jones is called the father of the quarterback sack. He was part of the Los Angeles Rams' "Fearsome Foursome" defensive line in the 1960s. Jones even added the term "sack" to the NFL vocabulary.

"You know, like you sack a city," Jones said. "You devastate it."

Jack Lambert was a key component in Pittsburgh's Steel Curtain defenses of the 1970s.

Mike Singletary directed traffic in the middle of the great Chicago Bears defenses of the 1980s.

The Fearsome Foursome started a trend. In the 1970s, many strong defenses had tough nicknames. The Cowboys had the Doomsday Defense. The Purple People Eaters stalked the tundra in Minnesota. Pittsburgh slammed down the Steel Curtain. Denver Broncos fans roared for the Orange Crush. And the No-Name Defense in Miami didn't sound scary—until you saw how it manhandled the opposition.

And for years, the Chicago Bears defense was known as "The Monsters of the Midway." The 1985 team, led by Hall of Fame linebacker Mike Singletary, was one of the most dominant defenses in NFL history.

Lots of players had cool nicknames, too. Star cornerback Deion Sanders had two: "Prime Time" and "Neon Deion." Sanders was the NFL's best pass defender throughout the 1990s. He also played receiver and returned kicks.

Defensive end Reggie White was known as the "Minister of Defense." He left the Eagles for Green Bay in 1993. Then he helped the Packers win their first Super Bowl since the 1960s.

Randy White of the Cowboys was a rugged defensive tackle. He was known as "Manster"—half man, half monster. Teammate Ed "Too Tall" Jones was, indeed, tall: 6 feet 9 inches, to be precise.

IT'S A BLITZ!

One of a defense's most exciting plays is the blitz. It happens when more than the usual four linemen rush the passer. Some teams will send as many as seven players on a blitz. The goal is to make the quarterback throw before he wants to.

Joe Greene of the Steelers was nicknamed "Mean Joe." But only players trying to block the massive defensive tackle found him to be mean. Meanwhile, defensive end Bruce Smith is the only player with 200 sacks since it became an official statistic in 1982. Smith and the Bills won four straight AFC championships in the early 1990s. Lawrence Taylor of the Giants made the strip-sack a part of football. He would tackle a quarterback while also knocking the ball loose.

One of today's biggest defensive stars is defensive end J. J. Watt of the Houston Texans. Watt won the NFL Defensive Player of the Year Award three times between 2012 and 2015.

Safety Paul Krause retired in 1979 with a record 81 interceptions.

J. J. Watt terrorizes opposing quarterbacks for the Houston Texans.

8 CHAMPIONSHIP COACHES

Great players need smart coaches to help them win. The Hall of Fame is filled with those coaches. They go all the way back to when football was just getting started as a sport.

Amos Alonzo Stagg was the coach at the University of Chicago from 1892 to 1932. He was credited with many innovations that changed the game. They include the huddle, the center snap, and the forward pass. Stagg coached until he was 96 years old.

Vince Lombardi, *left*, and George Halas were two of the greatest coaches in NFL history.

Walter Camp was known as "The Father of American Football." His ideas for the game included limiting teams to 11 players per side and putting numbers on jerseys. He is also credited with the scoring system of six points for a touchdown, three for a field goal, and two for a safety. Knute Rockne turned Notre Dame into a college power in the 1920s. He helped make the passing game popular.

POP WARNER

Pop Warner was one of the great teachers in football. He coached at six different colleges between 1895 and 1939. Warner brought the spiral pass and spiral punt to the game. He invented the double-wing formation to help with blocking. He also loved running trick plays. The biggest youth football league in America today is named for Warner.

As the NFL became more popular, it also had star coaches. Chicago Bears owner George Halas coached his team for 40 seasons. Halas won 324 games and six championships. Curly Lambeau led the Green Bay Packers to six titles between 1929 and 1944. Then Vince Lombardi took them from the bottom of the league to five championships in the 1960s.

Bill Walsh, *left*, and Joe Montana won three Super Bowls together with the 49ers.

Lombardi's Packers won the first two Super Bowls. The Super Bowl trophy is named after Lombardi.

In the Super Bowl era, Chuck Noll built Pittsburgh's tough Steel Curtain defense. He coached the Steelers to four titles in six seasons in the 1970s. Next came Bill Walsh and his West Coast offense with the 49ers. San Francisco won four Super Bowls in the 1980s, three with Walsh in charge.

Joe Gibbs won three Super Bowls with three different starting quarterbacks in Washington. The Patriots and Bill Belichick won their fourth championship, all with Tom Brady as quarterback, after the 2014 season.

9

HEATED RIVALRIES

Fans get most excited about games against their top rivals. Some are in-state college series such as the Iron Bowl (Alabama-Auburn) or Bedlam (Oklahoma-Oklahoma State). Others are border wars such as Michigan-Ohio State or Florida-Georgia. Those games often are played at the end of the season, adding to the drama.

Few games in sports are more revered than the annual Army-Navy meeting each December. The president of the United States sometimes goes to

The Army-Navy football rivalry is one of the oldest in the nation.

Floyd of Rosedale is a traveling trophy that goes to the winner of the Minnesota-Iowa game.

the game. The commander in chief traditionally sits on the Army side for one half and the Navy side for the other.

NFL rivalries often are based on divisional matchups. These teams play twice every year. Miami and New York City are not close to each other, but the Dolphins and Jets are major rivals in the AFC East. The same goes for Kansas City and Oakland in the AFC West. Dallas and Washington are longtime NFC East foes.

The oldest rivalry in the NFL is the one between Chicago and Green Bay. As part of the NFC North, they play twice a year. But their series goes back to 1921. Through the 2015 season, they had faced each other 192 times. Chicago led the series 94–92 with six ties.

Making that rivalry more special, the Packers (13) and Bears (9) have won more NFL titles than any other teams.

COLLEGE TROPHIES

In many college football rivalries, the winner gets to take a great trophy back to its campus. The oldest is the Little Brown Jug. This goes to the winner of the Minnesota-Michigan game. Floyd of Rosedale, a bronze statue shaped like a pig, is on the line when Iowa plays Minnesota. Indiana and Purdue play for the Old Oaken Bucket. The Apple Cup is up for grabs between Washington and Washington State. Nevada-Las Vegas battles rival Nevada for the Fremont Cannon.

10

THE DRAFT

NFL teams once bid against each other to sign college players coming into the league. In 1936 the league held its first draft. The teams took turns selecting players, starting with the club that had the worst record the year before.

The first draft took place in a Philadelphia hotel ballroom. Chicago chose Heisman Trophy winner Jay Berwanger. Berwanger said he didn't want to play pro football. And he never did.

Still, the idea made sense. The draft became a way to level the playing field. It gave the worst

Former NFL commissioner Pete Rozelle at the 1970 NFL Draft

Round 1
NO.
CLUB
PITTSBURGH
GREEN BAY
TERRY
MIKE
PHIL
AL
STEVE

BARGAIN PICK

Every year fans argue about who was the "steal of the draft." They're talking about the best player chosen with a late-round pick. But there's really no argument over who was the all-time steal of the draft. It has to be New England's sixth-round pick, No. 199 overall, in 1999: Tom Brady. The quarterback from Michigan became a starter in 2001 and won the Super Bowl that year. Brady led the Patriots to three more NFL championships through 2015. He is a surefire Hall of Famer.

teams the first shot at the best of the available young talent entering the league. Teams that drafted well could improve their record quickly.

ESPN televised the draft for the first time in 1980. Soon more and more fans began tuning in. The draft itself became big business. It went from one day of picks to two days and now three. It moved from hotels to theaters so fans could buy tickets and attend. Some fans come to the draft dressed in team jerseys or in costumes. They cheer some picks but boo others.

The star players attend the draft with their families and friends. Before the draft they walk

Cowboys running back Ezekiel Elliott, *left*, snaps a selfie with NFL commissioner Roger Goodell at the 2016 NFL Draft.

the red carpet like they're at a Hollywood movie premiere. When their names are announced, they walk onto the stage and hug NFL Commissioner Roger Goodell. Then they pose with a hat or a jersey from their new team. It's the first step on the path to their new career.

HALLS OF FAME

The best of the best in football usually end up in the Hall of Fame. The Pro Football Hall of Fame is located in Canton, Ohio. The College Football Hall of Fame is in Atlanta, Georgia.

The halls are fun places to learn about the history of the game. They feature the players, coaches, owners, and others who did great things. Hands-on displays let fans call plays, act as a referee, and even play video games.

One of the highlights of the college hall is a wall displaying more than 700 helmets. Visitors can play

The College Football Hall of Fame opened a new building in Atlanta in 2014.

Members of the Pro Football Hall of Fame class of 2013 stand with their busts.

catch or kick the ball around on a small-scale field. And they can learn all about the players and coaches who have been inducted to the hall.

Members of the Pro Football Hall of Fame are honored with busts in Canton. A bust is a statue of a person's head, shoulders, and sometimes the upper part of the chest. Visitors can read all about the giants of pro football at this exhibit. The hall also displays memorabilia from big games and record-breaking feats.

The Hall of Fame Game is played at the stadium next to the hall in Canton. It's always the first game of the preseason. One of the teams usually has a player or coach from its past who is being inducted that year. A big celebration is held the night before the game. This is when the new members are inducted into the hall. The next night, the game represents the unofficial kickoff to the new season.

CANTON, OHIO

The first professional football league started in Canton, Ohio, in 1920. It was called the American Professional Football Association (APFA). One of its teams was the Canton Bulldogs. The APFA became the National Football League in 1922. The Bulldogs won the NFL championship in 1922 and 1923. The team folded in 1926. The Pro Football Hall of Fame opened in 1963.

12 PLAYING FOOTBALL

The sport might be called *football*, but it's played with the hands as much as with the feet. And there are so many different ways to play it.

In NFL and college games, 11 players on offense battle with 11 players on defense. Most high schools also have 22 players on the field at once. But many smaller high schools play with fewer than 11 players per side. In Texas more than 200 high schools play "six-man" football.

In tackle football, defenders try to get the ball carrier down to the ground. In touch football, simply

A flag football player runs with the ball.

touching the person with the ball brings the play to an end. In flag football, players wear belts with two or three strips of fabric attached to them, usually with Velcro. A defensive player needs to tear one of the ball carrier's flags off the belt to end a play.

EXTRA POINTS

In 2015 the NFL moved the line of scrimmage for extra-point kicks to the 15-yard line. Previously teams snapped the ball from the 2-yard line. Those kicks were almost automatic for a pro kicker. In 2014 NFL teams made 99.3 percent of their extra-point kicks. The next year, kicking from the longer distance, the conversion rate dropped to 94.2 percent.

Other rules are generally the same across all levels. The team with the ball must gain 10 yards in four tries, or downs, to keep an offensive drive going. If one team crosses the goal line into the end zone with the ball, it's a touchdown. That's worth six points. The scoring team can then run a play from near the goal line for two points. Or, it can attempt a one-point kick.

You also can score without reaching the end zone. The team with the ball can kick it through

A reliable placekicker is a must for a championship team.

the uprights at the back of the end zone. That's a field goal, and it's worth three points. When a team is trapped with the football in its own end zone, it's a safety. That's worth two points. Teams can run with the ball or pass it to move downfield. But only one forward pass is allowed per play. And it must come from behind the line of scrimmage.

GLOSSARY

draft
A system that allows teams to acquire new players coming into a league.

end zone
The end of the field where teams try to score touchdowns.

fumble
When a player with the ball loses possession, allowing the opponent a chance to recover it.

huddle
Where players on a team's offense and defense each meet on the field to call plays.

interception
When a defensive player catches a pass intended for an offensive player.

lateral
A pass that goes sideways or backward.

line of scrimmage
The place on the field where a play starts.

poll
A survey of people's opinions on a subject. Polls of college football coaches and media are used to rank teams.

scrambled
Ran around with the ball behind the line of scrimmage while looking for an open receiver.

snap
The start of each play, when the center hikes the ball between his legs to a player behind him, usually the quarterback.

FOR MORE INFORMATION

Books

Anastasio, Dina. *What Is The Super Bowl?* New York: Grosset and Dunlap, 2015.

Jacobs, Greg. *The Everything Kids' Football Book.* Avon, Massachusetts: Adams Media, 2014.

Kelley, K. C. *Football Superstars 2015.* New York: Scholastic Inc. Publishers, 2015.

Websites

To learn more about football, visit booklinks.abdopublishing.com. These links are routinely monitored and updated to provide the most current information available.

INDEX

ABOUT THE AUTHOR

Barry Wilner is the pro football writer for the Associated Press and has covered every Super Bowl since 1987. He has written more than 55 books. He teaches journalism and communications at Manhattanville College. He lives in Garnerville, New York.